Everything

Anglo Jewish Women

Need to Know

About Divorce

In Israel

JAY HAIT, ADV.

www.IsraeldivorceLawyer.com

ISBN-10: 1540864324
ISBN-13: 978-1540864321

Including

- 4 issues that have to be addressed for every Jewish couple with children getting divorced in Israel
- 3 things you have to know regarding which court will hear your divorce issues – Family court or Rabbinic court
- 11 Tips for living in the same house with your husband prior to the divorce
- 7 rules you must follow with the social worker evaluating who will get custody
- 3 determinants needed to calculate child support
- Over 20 Financial records you should be gathering
- 20 steps to prepare for a divorce
- 16 Questions you should be asking about your attorney
- 7 stages of divorce
- 43 age appropriate books about divorce for children in English

WARNING AND DISCLAIMER

The goal of this book is to provide general information, and not to render specific legal advice.

Please use this book for informational purposes only.

For specific advice about your situation you should speak to a qualified divorce attorney.

RECOMMENDED PRACTICES TO UTILIZE THIS BOOK

Believe it or not, a lot of people who have read my informational materials have later spoken to me and told me that the information I have given them is great, but that many times they have gotten into "information overload" and failed to utilize the information they received. To people like this, I have two pieces of advice. The first piece of advice is to read and re-read. Many times you will find that by re-reading the same material more than once that the information is internalized even without your consciously trying to memorize things. The second piece of advice that I give them is to take notes, and in the case of books – even right in the book itself. I know that many of us have such a great respect for books that we would never write in a book. At most, many of us would highlight important texts (do you remember doing that in college or graduate school?), but we would never actually write in a book. <u>Throw out that mentality when you read this book</u>. This book is meant to help you. This book is meant to be written in. Write in the sides of the book. Highlight text that speaks to you. Jot down notes in the notes section of the book that starts on page 85. The important thing is to not just read this information and forget about it – but to utilize the information to help yourself to come to a decision about which direction you want your life to continue in. Whether you decide to get divorced in the end or not, you should do whatever it takes to understand and internalize the information in this book. As the saying goes "knowledge is power." But not knowledge that is just sitting on the bookshelf...

Jay Hait, Adv.

Special Note about Hebrew language conventions utilized throughout this book

Although my office does everything possible to help our Anglo clients to go through the divorce process in their native tongue, we cannot simply ignore the fact that we are living in Israel and that the official language in the court system is Hebrew. To that end, throughout this book when we introduce legal terminology we will a) first use the English language word, 2) introduce the transliterated Hebrew term in English letters, 3) type the term in Hebrew, and 4) if the literal translation is different than the English language word, we will present the literal translation. After the initial usage we will either use the English terminology or the transliterated Hebrew terminology.

For example: Motion (in Hebrew bakasha בקשה) literally, a request.

Subsequent use throughout the book will be Motion or bakasha.

The reason that we do this is that in our opinion it is important that you are familiar with the Hebrew terminology both so that you will understand terminology utilized in the course of a divorce or negotiations, and secondly so that you understand the terminology utilized by third parties who you will be in contact with in the event of divorce (social workers, professionals, and even family and friends).

Special Note about facts and statistics sprinkled throughout this book

Most of the facts and statistics that you will find on the sidelines throughout this book (referred to as Jay's factoids by some of my office staff) are statistics that I find come across from time to time either on the Israeli government's Central Bureau of Statistics website, the Rabbinic court's website, newspaper articles, or different studies that I read on occasion. I share them with you just because I find them interesting, although there is no guarantee that they are one hundred percent accurate, and hope that you do too.

Special Note about url (uniform resource locators – or in the vernacular, web addresses) links sprinkled throughout this book

Everybody learns things differently. Some people absorb information better when they read it. Some people absorb information better when they hear it. Some people absorb information better when they see it in video format. Throughout this book I have listed links to different urls with information that I have created in other formats (usually video – I love making educational videos) that may be of interest to you and may help you to better absorb the information that I am sharing with you in this book. Visit the sites if you are interested, but even if you don't, most if not all of the same information will be covered in the print version of this book.

ACKNOWLEDGMENTS

The last thirteen years of my life have been incredibly different than the thirty some odd prior to that. I have found the strength to "go against the tide" and to just do things because I thought of them and wanted to do them or to at least try to do them. All of this because of the support and backing of my life partner and wife Anat. Without her support and encouragement I never would have actually written a book to help the many women we find stuck in unhappy marriages here in Israel – even though for years I have been saying that somebody ought to write a guide for them.

Thank you to my all of my staff throughout the years that I have been practicing law in Israel. Not only have you have helped me to learn and to implement the law here in Israel, but you have also taught me to navigate and to understand both my adopted culture and the mentality of my fellow Israelis and to understand how it all plays out in the family law legal system.

Contents

WHO IS THE AUTHOR OF THIS BOOK AND WHY SHOULD I LISTEN TO HIM?

Take a deep breathe. Sit back. Relax. Everything is going to be okay. The thought of getting divorced may be daunting and even overwhelming. The thought of having to go through such an emotional process in Hebrew may seem unsurmountable. Additionally, you are probably having thoughts like "How will I be able to pay for everything? What is going to happen to my kids? Where are we going to live? How is he going to react? What will my parents and family say? Can I make it on my own?" Slow down and take things one step at a time. Time and again we have seen women come through the process stronger, happier, more in control of their lives and their futures, and with a feeling of freedom and of having been relieved of excess baggage which had been limiting them, suffocating them, and holding them back.

> **Did you know?**
> Roughly 40,000 couples a year in Israel get married and about 11,000 get divorced?

If you are a woman considering divorce, or if your husband has started the divorce process, just be aware that you don't have to go through it alone. Help, guidance, and information to enable you to empower yourself is available. You have to know the

3

different procedures involved in going through your divorce, and how the divorce process in Israel works.

You need to understand that there are professionals able and willing to help you to organize your life into manageable parts in order to make your divorce less overwhelming; and that by having an understanding of the laws and procedures that govern divorce in Israel you will relieve a large part of the stress associated with divorce.

My name is Jay Hait. I am an American Israeli attorney licensed in both the United States and in Israel. I have been practicing law for almost two decades, and my Israeli practice focuses solely on family law (divorce negotiation, divorce litigation, divorce mediation, wills, trusts, and estates). When I first moved to Israel in 2004, I continued to fly back and forth to New York City to continue to work there in my corporate law practice. However, I started practicing in the family law field because I found myself where you are now. I was in an unhappy marriage. In the end – since I didn't have the knowledge that you will gain by reading this book – things simply spun out of control. Multiple lawsuits were litigated in multiple countries. Too much money was spent litigating points that shouldn't have been litigated. At the end of the day I found myself as the longest open Agun* in the Israeli court system (and yes – there are Agunim in Israel as well as Agunote – although nobody debates the fact that the consequences are much worse for the Agunah than for the Agun). I found myself with my now ex-wife living in the United States and not even visiting my three children (who ended up growing up with me in Israel) for almost six years due to her attorney's lousy advice. Simply put: an unmitigated disaster for all parties.

> **Did you know?**
> Divorced men get are two times more likely to get married a second time than divorced women.

I opened my family law practice – and am now writing this book – to show you that this is not the way it has to be, nor should it. Divorce sucks. However, being in a bad marriage is even worse. Worse for you. Worse for your spouse. Worse for your children. In my family law practice we attempt to create teams and groups of professionals to assist in educating and representing people to wade through the divorce process with confidence and support. We know, and help our clients to understand, that information becomes power, and we empower our clients by giving them the information and the tools that they need in order to maximize their legal rights throughout the divorce process. Most importantly, we help them to do this without turning their divorces into scorched earth World War III scenarios whereby their children turn out to be the biggest casualties.

In our office, our mission is to change the dynamic of how people are represented and treated by their attorneys throughout the divorce process. We understand that women facing divorce are confronting a challenging time in their lives and can get caught up with confusing

For more information on divorce in Israel, visit http://34.gs/Divorce411.

emotions and conflicting loyalties. We find that at this point in their lives, most women are trying to deal with and acclimate to the concept of change – for themselves, for their children, for their extended family, and for their friends.

This book will not solve all of your problems, but it will give you a wealth of information and provide you with the tools that you need to address your divorce related issues in an educated, intelligent manner in order to maximize the results of your divorce.

OUR GUARANTEE

You are in the right place at the right time. By reading this book, you are going to become empowered, because you will have the answers to more Israeli divorce-related questions than most women even ask. You will probably know more about divorce in Israel not only than your husband, but than the vast majority of the men who live in Israel.

SO LET'S BEGIN!

---

*Agun/ah (m/f) – literally somebody who has been chained. Under Israeli (and Jewish) law, it is a person whose spouse has been unwilling to grant them or accept from them a religious writ of divorce (a Get) – usually in order to exact financial benefit or emotional revenge.

THE BASICS – A SYSTEMATIC OVERVIEW OF THE DIVORCE PROCESS IN ISRAEL

In divorce in Israel – any divorce – there are a number of factors that ultimately must be resolved.

1. If there are children – who will have custody over the children and what will the visitation schedule be for the non-custodial parent?

2. If there are children – and if the mother has custody over them - what is the amount of monthly child support that will be paid?

   Did you know?
   In 2015 11,114 couples got divorced in the Rabbinic courts as opposed to 11,023 in 2014 – a rise of less than one percent.

3. How will the assets and debts of the divorcing couple be split?

Furthermore, in the event that both of the parties (i.e. both the wife and the husband) are considered Jewish by Jewish law, there is a fourth factor:

4. The Jewish writ of divorce (in Hebrew, Get גט),
   sometimes referred to as the body of the divorce itself.

It is important to understand that these are the basic factors that
need to be addressed in every Israeli divorce between Jewish
spouses. Further, because they embody the issues that need to
be addressed in every Israeli divorce between Jewish spouses,
and because their outcomes can be affected by which court
addresses which of these issues, it is important to have a basic
understanding of how the system works.

Before we continue, it is very important for you to understand
something regarding the 4th issue –
the Get. Many people think that if
they weren't married according to
Jewish tradition (in Hebrew,
Halacha הלכה), and that if they got
married outside of Israel in a secular
ceremony, then they will not have to
go through the Get process.
Unfortunately, this is not generally
the case. As long as both the wife
and the husband are considered Jewish according to Jewish law
(as determined by the Rabbinic court (in Hebrew, Bet Din בית
דין) literally, house of law) then in order for the couple to get
divorced in Israel they will have to go through the Get process.

> **Did you know?**
> The percentage of
> couples in Israel from the
> FSU that get divorced is
> significantly higher than
> the percentage of
> couples in the general
> population.

Now that we know what the issues are that need to be
addressed in Israeli divorces, let's look at where all of these
things get adjudicated (heard).

In Israel, there are two court systems which have simultaneous
jurisdiction over the four divorce issues detailed above – or at
least some of them. What this means is that two different court
systems – the secular Family court (in Hebrew, Bet HaMishpat
LaInyanei Mishpacha בית המשפט לעניני משפחה) literally, the

family affairs court, and the religious Rabbinic court - can end up being the court in which some of the divorce issues are decided. In the Family court, a single judge presides at the hearings and makes decisions. In the Rabbinic court, a panel of three Rabbinic court judges (in Hebrew, Dayanim דייני) presides and makes the decisions. Which court hears the case determines which law will be applied (i.e. Jewish law or secular law) and can therefore affect the outcome of the case. Even though in theory the Family court is also supposed to rule within the confines of Jewish law in these cases (i.e. divorces between two Jewish spouses), in practice the Family court's application and interpretation of Jewish law can differ greatly from that of the Rabbinic court. Whoever brings the appropriate suit in front of the appropriate court first determines which court will decide of that issue. This is the cause for what is referred to as

You can see a video on the race for jurisdiction in Israel by going to http://s87.eu/race.

the "race for jurisdiction". In laymen's terms, what it means is that historically, people would rush to bring divorce related suits before their spouse brought the suit, because that would enable them to determine which court upon their issues and which law is applied.

In theory, this "race for jurisdiction" was supposed to change with a new law that went into effect last summer which obligates divorcing parties to go through a form of social worker organized mediation. The social worker organized mediation begins when either the husband or the wife submits a Motion to Settle Differences (in Hebrew, Bakasha LiYashev Sichsooch

You can learn more about this mediation process via a complimentary mini video course that I made at http://s87.eu/mediation-course.

בקשה, ליישב סכסוך), which is really just a form and not a formal motion, with either the Rabbinic or Family courts. In reality the race for jurisdiction still exists because if the sides do not reach an agreement via the social worker organized mediation, then the side that made the motion first is able to decide which court will hear the issues between the parties via filing suit at the end of the mediation period.

There is one basic caveat however – neither court system has the power to make all of the decisions regarding all four of the factors that must be resolved. In a word, there are 3 basic things that you need to know about which court can hear which issues.

1. The Rabbinic court is the sole authority in Israel that is able to issue the Get – and thereby to legally end the marriage. So even if all of the other issues of your divorce are litigated (or much better - a comprehensive divorce agreement is affirmed) in the Family court, you still will not be divorced until you and your spouse have gone through the Get ceremony in the Rabbinic court. **This means that even if one side sues in the Family court first, the Get issue will always be done or decided in the Rabbinic court.**

2. Unless both parties agree that the Rabbinic court will have jurisdiction (i.e. will hear these issues) then the issue of child support payments will always be heard before the Family court. The reason for this is that child support is the right of the children, and via the person who has custody over them, they can always ask the Family court to make decisions regarding them - regardless of which jurisdiction their parents are litigating their other issues in. **This means that even if one side sues in the Family court first, the child support issue can always be decided in the Family court.**

3. Finally, either the Rabbinic court or the Family court can make decisions regarding a) who will have custody over minor children and what the visitation schedule with the non-custodial parent, and b) how the assets and debts of the couple will be divided. **This means that whoever brings a lawsuit for custody or for the division of assets first, can determine which court will be hearing those issues.**

It may be easier to understand by looking at the chart below:

Which court system can hear divorce issues in Israel?

	Family Court Jurisdiction	Rabbinic Court Jurisdiction
Custody	✓	✓
Division of Assets & Debts	✓	✓
Child Support Payments	✓	✓ - only if both sides agree
The "Get"		✓

Again, in areas where both courts have the ability to hear cases involving particular divorce issues, the spouse who brings the lawsuit first will determine which court will hear those issues, whether it is before or after the obligatory social worker coordinated mediation period.

Finally, you should understand that in the event of litigation you may be involved in multiple lawsuits when you get divorced. In the Rabbinic courts, all of the issues can be addressed in one lawsuit – let's call it "A Lawsuit for Divorce including Division of Assets and Custody (and if there is no Opposition then also for Child Support)." In the Family court each issue is addressed by a different lawsuit – one for division of assets, one for custody, and one for child support. (Remember – the divorce itself or the Get – can only be done in the Rabbinic courts). Usually what happens is that some issues are litigated in front of each court. Generally, we counsel our clients that the Get in the Rabbinic courts only be taken care of after all of the other issues have been resolved – either via a compromise agreement or judicial decision – whether from the Family or Rabbinic courts.

You can learn more about which court can hear which litigation issues by watching my video on how to start divorce suits in Israel at http://s87.eu/start-divorce.

Now that you have a basic understanding of the framework within which the divorce process in Israel works, let's dig into the particulars..

PRELIMINARY NOTE REGARDING ISRAEL'S "OBLIGATORY DIVORCE MEDIATION" LAW

A new law, effective July 2016, which many people have called Israel's "Obligatory divorce mediation" law – in Hebrew the Chok LeHesderei Hitdayanut Bisichsuchei Mishpacah *חוק להסדרי התדיינות בסכסוכי משפחה* (literally the "law for judicial procedures in family disputes"), changes the manner in which we start divorce litigation, but not its substantive issues.

Lots of people have approached me saying that they heard that as of July 2016, before a couple can get divorced in Israel, they have to go through obligatory mediation. Wrong. Although the new law has yet to be adjudicated (in other words – it still has to be interpreted by judges in lawsuits to see exactly how things are going to work out), in general what the law does is to organize divorce related lawsuits (and other certain suits – but those are not the subject of this book) in the following manner:

> Did you know?
> Parents of minor children get divorced less often than parents of post adolescent and adult children.

Spouse A files a Bakasha LiYashev Sichsuch that notifies either the Family court or the Rabbinic court (whichever court that

spouse elects to notify) that they are in dispute with Spouse B.
At that point a 45 day freeze occurs during which neither side
can bring a lawsuit against the other spouse – and can only
make emergency requests from either the Rabbinic or Family
courts (e.g. like a request for the court to prevent the other
spouse from abandoning them in Israel).

The sides are invited to an initial meeting with a social worker
connected to the court the form was filed in. The social worker
tries to evaluate the sides and the "story" at this meeting – and
then the social worker recommends to the couple how they can
continue – either by having more meetings (up to four) with the
social worker, going to marital
therapy, going to mediation, or
going through divorce via the
courts. Meetings with the social
worker are not charged for.
Meetings with professionals other
than the social worker will generally
be paid for by the couple. The
initial meeting with the social worker
is without either side's attorney present – although both spouses
are able to speak with their attorneys via telephone. If there are
follow up meetings with the social worker, each side may have
their attorney present.

Did you know?
In the United States, 41%
of first marriages end in
divorce, 60% of second
marriages end in divorce,
and 73% of third
marriages end in divorce.

After 45 days (or a longer period if both sides of the couple
agree to it) then the person who filed the form with the court
can bring lawsuits against their spouse within a 15 day period.
There is a lot more minutiae to the system, and if you are
interested to learn about it, I invite you to sign up for my
complimentary mini video course on the subject at
http://s87.eu/mediation-course.

The bottom line is that the law does open a potential path for
mediation, and that may end up being a good thing. However,

as I advised when they asked for comments on the law, it will also potentially force beaten women to sit across the table with their abusive husbands without an attorney to protect them but relying on the social worker. We will see what happens as the law is implemented....

LET'S GET STARTED – IS IT TRUE THAT THERE IS NO SUCH THING AS SEPARATION IN ISRAEL?

Many times women who start the divorce process ask me:

How do I get rid of him?

In Israel, unlike most other Western democratic countries, there is <u>no legal concept</u> of separation prior to divorce. This is a problem, because for most women, once they have decided that they are going to get divorced, the first thing that they want to do is to physically separate – i.e. they want their husband to leave the marital home or they want to leave themselves. While we understand this desire, and even more so the emotions that lead to this feeling, it is important to understand that barring either a judicial (from a court) or police order, that this is not going to happen at the initial stage. No judge is likely to throw your husband out of the house at the very beginning of the divorce process. You are not going to just pick up and leave the house because this can affect your legal rights regarding custody. The police will only remove your husband if he is a threat to you or your children. **DO NOT**

> **Did you know?**
> Couples where both parties are from the same country get divorced less than those couples that are "mixed"

MAKE FALSE ALLEGATIONS TO THE POLICE IN AN ATTEMPT TO HAVE HIM REMOVED. Besides the fact that this is immoral and illegal, while this might work in the short term, in many cases it will backfire in the long term. Bottom line – adjust accordingly for now – he is going to be in the house for the time being, and so are you.

You may be wondering – why can't I kick him out of the house? He's making both me and the kids miserable!

Nothing is more unsettling than when you are in the process of divorcing and you want your husband out of the house. Neither the police not the courts will remove anybody at this stage unless there is clear evidence of physical threats. You must keep your eye on the long term bigger picture. This situation is not going to go on for too long, and in the end you will no longer be living with him. He may be trying to make you miserable in an attempt to get you to leave the house – either with the kids, or even worse – without them. This can affect your legal rights. Don't do it! You should never leave the house until you have gotten the appropriate legal counsel as to when and how you should leave (if at all), and not without a clear strategy that you and your legal counsel agree to. Throughout this book I will be using the term legal counsel because if litigation is only occurring in the Rabbinic court then you may be represented by somebody who is not an attorney but a Religious Court Paralegal (in Hebrew, To-ane Rabbani טוען רבני) literally a Rabbinic claimer.

> **Did you know?**
> Female olim make up more than one third of the divorced women in

How can you adjust while you are living in the same home with your husband?

Understand that once the divorce process begins, your spouse may be getting legal advice that would enable him to "game the system" to get the best results for him. A classic example of this would be to have a divorce suit (e.g. in the Rabbinic court) dismissed because you and he were having marital relations after the suit had been filed. Israeli law recognizes something called the date of irreconcilable differences (in Hebrew, Ta'areech HaKera *תעריך הקרע*) literally, "the date of the rip." This is the date after which it is clear that the parties are not reconciling. This date can affect your legal rights. For example, if you receive an inheritance after this date, it will be

almost impossible for him to make a claim on those assets assuming that you have taken the proper steps. During the period while it is clear that you are divorcing but are not yet divorced and while your husband is still living in the marital household, we recommend that you take the following steps:

1. Do not sleep in the same bedroom as him. If he insists on sleeping in your bedroom, sleep on the couch, in one of the kids' rooms, or in the guest room or office.

2. Do not fool around or have intimate relations with him.

3. Do not go out with him socially.

4. Do not eat meals with him except for the Sabbath (in Hebrew, Shabbat *שבת*) and holidays or children's birthdays where you are eating meals with the whole family.

5. Use a separate and secure computer.

6. Use a separate and secure telephone.

7. Open a separate banking account.

8. When you have small children, only attend events that are vital together: e.g. parent teacher conferences, doctor appointments, etc.

9. Cease to give your spouse gifts for holidays and birthdays.

10. If he or you have already filed for divorce, let people (i.e. friends and family, co-workers) know that you are getting divorced and are only living together temporarily until things are sorted out, and not as husband and wife.

11. Do not hold yourselves out as "the happy couple" in front of neighbors and friends.

All of the above are important. Some of the things listed are important because they safeguard personal or private information that could be used against you, and some of the things listed are important because they help to solidify and clarify for the court (whether family or Rabbinic) what your intent is. The bottom line is however, that all of these things will help your case to move to a close sooner rather than later, which will make the time that you will be living together shorter.

Did you know?
The average age of people who get married for the first time in Israel is 27.6 for men (27.8 amongst Jews) and 24.8 for women (25.7 amongst Jews).

SHOULD YOU BE THE FIRST TO FILE?

I always tell my female clients that if they fear that their husband will be filing suit, and/or if they want to get temporary child support that they should be filing first. There are a couple of reasons for this. The first reason, in the case of fear that the husband will file first, is that you will want to sue in the court which will maximize the potential legal outcome for you. Many people think that this means "women should file in the Family court and men should file in the Rabbinic court." This is not always the case. For example if a woman owns a business, she should probably be filing for division of assets in the Rabbinic court and not in the Family court. This would not prevent her from also filing for custody in the Family court at the same time.

The second reason to file first, in the case of temporary child support, is twofold. Understand that temporary child support is a motion brought as part of a general suit for child support. On the **strategic level**, filing first for temporary child support send a loud and clear message to your husband "You are not in control anymore." It lets him know that the playing field has been revamped and that he will have to deal with your lawyer and not with you if he intends to play games with money from here on. It lets him know that a judge will be calling the shots.

On the **tactical level,** it lets you tell your story first. Your lawyer, representing your interests, gets to tell the judge(s) (whether in the Family court or the Rabbinic court) the facts the way you see them before they anybody hears your husband's view of things. I find that having the first word when filing temporary child support motions leads to better results for my clients.

Did you know?
Men who have open heart surgery while they are married are three times more likely to survive for three months after the operation than single or divorced men, and 2.5 times more likely to survive for at least five years after the operation than single or divorced men.

I do not view this as changing much with the new law in place – just that now I tell my female clients that if they fear that their husband will be filing suit, and/or if they want to get temporary child support that they should be filing the Bakasha LaYashev Sichsuch first – so that when the time comes for filing lawsuits (if required) they have the first right of refusal to do so, and they can determine what case is heard and in front of which court.

WHAT IS THE DIVORCE PROCESS?

Let's assume that your husband just left. Maybe you had a fight. Maybe you've just been unhappy with each other for a long time. Maybe he has started dating somebody and is having an affair. Whatever it is, you have decided that your marriage has come to an end and that you are going to file for divorce. What usually happens at this stage is that you hire an attorney, and after coming up with a legal strategy together with him or her, and after going through the social worker initiated process oftentimes misquoted as the "obligatory divorce mediation law", you prepare one or more documents that are known as complaints (in Hebrew, Kitvei Tvia כתבי תביעה). How many complaints are filed depend on which court you are filing in, and what you are filing for. Generally, when we represent the wife, our clients file between two and three complaints. For example we may file a complaint in the Rabbinic court for divorce and division of assets and custody

> ### Did you know?
> The main reasons for divorce amongst Orthodox Jews in Israel: marriage at too young an age or without having known the spouse for a long enough time; having become parents at too young an age; and lastly, spouses having hidden pertinent information from them prior to marriage (usually regarding medical conditions or legal problems).

over minor children; and at the same time we would file in the family court for child support. Another example would be that we would file three separate suits in the Family court for custody; for child support; and for the division of assets. When we file these three cases in the Family court we generally do not file for divorce in the Rabbinic court – as we find that once these three issues have been adjudicated that the husband is willing to go to the Rabbinic court for the Get ceremony without our client incurring the costs of filing an additional suit for divorce in the Rabbinic court. Each of the complaints contains basic information about the couple: their names and Israeli ID numbers; when they married and where; how the parties got to where they are in their relationship; for some of the complaints – children's names, birth dates and Israeli Id numbers; and most importantly what it is that our client wants the court to give them. You will generally sign an affidavit for each complaint affirming the truth of everything stated in the complaint, and you will sign a power of attorney enabling your attorney to

> **Did you know?**
> In the last 15 years the number of people that have married for a second time in Israel has gone down by 33%.

submit and receive documents on your behalf. The complaints will be filed in the appropriate Family and/or Rabbinic courts depending upon which city you live in. At this point, for purposes of the courts, you are known as the plaintiff (in Hebrew, Tova'at תובעת) and your husband is known as the defendant (in Hebrew, Nitva נתבע) Hebrew.

After the relevant complaint(s) have been filed and the filing fees paid (filing fees may be as high as two to three thousand shekels depending on which complaints are brought, although some of those fees may be returned upon completion of the process), the court will either serve the papers on your husband or you will have a private process server serve him. In our office we generally use a process server. The cost of this is usually only a few hundred shekels, but the sooner your husband is served the more quickly the divorce will start to take place. Remember that until your husband is served the divorce litigation hasn't really started. Once he has been served your husband has between 30 to 45 days to respond to your complaints (depending on which court and which suit). His response is called an answer (in Hebrew, Ktav Hagana כתב הגנה), literally a letter of defense. Generally, in this period he may also bring counter suits against you, and may make motions to the court – but these are not things that you should be worried about – once you are in divorce litigation you are in divorce litigation, and no matter what the positioning your husband attempts to achieve – the bottom line is that the four issues referred to at the beginning of this book that must be addressed will remain the same. Remember, your husband may make allegations against you that are way over exaggerated. If this happens, don't let it intimidate you! Remember, your husband's attorney may be trying to intimidate or disturb you. He is creatively writing what he has been told and is trying to make you look as negative as possible. Either your husband or his attorney is trying to get under your skin and to push your buttons. Don't let them. The best thing to do is not to react – because they are expecting you to react. By not reacting you may actually throw them off of their game rather than you being thrown off of your game.

Did you know?
On average 1.6 people get divorced every year for every 1,000 people in the general population. Amongst Jews the number is 1.9 people, amongst Muslims it is 1 person, amongst Druze it is 0.8 people, and amongst Christians it is 0.3 people. These numbers have doubled since the 1960s – for all religions.

After this the court proceedings will begin. This generally entails one or more preliminary conferences at which the Family court judge or Rabbinical court dayanim will a) hear preliminary requests (motions), and b) try to get the sides to agree on at least some of the issues, and c) set timelines for the remainder of the case.

Once all of the pretrial issues have been dealt with the Family court judge or Rabbinical court dayanim panel will set one or more dates for evidentiary hearings. These hearings are what most westerners envision as a court date (the type of stuff you see on television). Here the parties are cross examined and evidence is presented.

> To learn more about the pretrial conference in the Family court you can watch the video at http://s87.eu/pretrial.

After the evidentiary hearing(s) are completed, there may or may not be oral or written summations (it is up to the Family court judge or Rabbinical court dayanim to decide if they want them and in what format), and then a written judgement is issued.

Again, it's important to remember that over ninety percent of cases never reach this stage and that at some earlier point (i.e. before a judgement is issued) the parties come to some sort of an agreement.

CAUSES FOR DIVORCE

If you haven't gotten the concept until now, another way that Israel is different from other Western countries when it comes to divorce is that most suits that start a divorce aren't divorce suits. They are lawsuits for the division of assets, for custody, and/or for child support. Yes, most of the people involved in those suits do end up getting divorced, but the initial suits aren't divorce suits. Also, remember – since only the Rabbinic court can issue the Get, the only court in which you can really bring a suit for "divorce" is in the Rabbinic court.

Why am I bringing this up? Why is it important for you to understand? Because in the event that either you or your spouse bring a suit for divorce in the Rabbinic courts (and again – this suit can include the division of assets, custody, and if you agree – child support) then you must have adequate legal grounds to sue for divorce. These legal grounds are defined in Halacha and Rabbinic case law. Some of the grounds are those known to us from popular television shows. Some are unique to Jewish law. Adultery, spousal abuse (physical or verbal), impotence and/or infertility, gambling, alcoholism,

Did you know?
Women are twice as likely to get divorced in a second marriage as in a first marriage.

unwillingness to have marital relations. All of these are some of the causes for divorce in the Rabbinic court. Here is an example of why it is important to understand this. In the event that your husband sues for divorce and/or division of assets and/or child custody in the Rabbinic court, and you want the issues of child custody and division of assets to be litigated in the Family court, then if you can prove that he does not have legal grounds for divorce, the case may be dismissed and you will have the ability to try to file suits over these issues in the Family court. It is far from a "sure thing" but it is possible.

It is also very important to understand the concept of intent when suits are brought in the Rabbinic court. A suit for divorce that is brought in the Rabbinic court by one of the spouses cannot continue if it is determined that the suit was brought in order to pressure the other side, but that there really was no intent to get divorced. I remember a case a few years ago where the case was dismissed on the spot because during one of the hearings the Rabbinic court judges found out that the couple was still having marital relations.

Finally, I wanted to address the issue (which is grounds for divorce) of the rebellious wife (in Hebrew, Eesha Moredet אישה מורדת). A woman who is determined by the Rabbinic court to be a rebellious wife may find that she 1) loses her right to be supported by her husband while they are still married, and 2) may lose her right to payments pursuant to the Jewish marriage contract (in Hebrew, Katoova כתובה) literally "writing" (the contract in Jewish law

> **Did you know?**
> The average Israeli family spends 15,053 NIS on goods and services, and the average family with children spends 4.1 times the average family without children.

which established the marriage). The payment the wife is entitled to is known as the Jewish marriage contract payment (in Hebrew, Dmei Katoova דמי כתובה). Remember, the Dmei

Katoova is only available to women who were married via a Jewish wedding and not to women who married civilly outside of Israel. In any case, you can be considered an Eesha Moredet if you unilaterally leave your home (but not if it's because he is physically abusing you), if you are caught having an affair, if you refuse to accept the Get from your husband, if you refuse to take care of your husband, etc. This is why when I represent the wife, I tell my clients time and again that they should not change care routines in the household prior to the divorce – i.e. even if you don't eat with your husband or spend much time with him because you just can't stand him, if you are the main food preparer in your household, continue to prepare food for him as well. If you are the main laundry cleaner in the household, continue to do his laundry too. I understand that it is aggravating to feel compelled to do these things when you are with one foot out the door of your marriage, but remember that this is a temporary situation and that it could influence the amount of money that you will ultimately be entitled to. Keep your eyes on the long term goal and not the short term aggravation.

THE CONCEPT OF FAULT

Almost everybody going through a divorce feels that it is the other side's fault. But what about fault in the eyes of the law and how can it affect the outcome of the divorce? Since Israeli divorces between Jewish spouses only occur in the Rabbinic court, the Halachic (Jewish law) concepts of grounds for divorce can include fault. However, on a practical level the legal concept of "fault" should have a minimal impact on the outcome of the divorce – at least with regards to finances.

In the Family court, the legal concept of fault is really irrelevant. With regards to assets the civil law states that somebody's poor behavior should not affect what assets he or she owns. With regards to children's custody the test in the court is "what is in the best interests of the child(ren)?" This is also the test with regards to child support.

Although in the past the Rabbinic courts have made rulings in the division of assets that allocated fault to the woman (for example in the case of an affair) and therefore the Rabbinic court did not give the wife fifty percent of the assets of the

Did you know?
Ninety five percent of the couples in Israel are married, and the other five percent are couples that live together

couple, the Supreme Court has reversed such rulings. What this means is that at the first level hearings, if you are in the Rabbinic courts, and the court rules against you because it is assigning you fault of some type, you should appeal. But again, the Rabbinic courts will rarely do this.

In the case of adultery it may influence the Rabbinic court's rulings on custody. Even though the golden rule regarding custody is supposed to be that the courts act in the best interest of the child(ren), in reality the Rabbinic courts do sometimes take into account either spouses bad behavior when balancing what is in the best interest of the child(ren).

THE TYPES OF REQUESTS THAT
THE COURTS CAN GRANT

In Israel, whether your divorce related matters are heard in the Rabbinic court or the Family court, there are certain types of temporary decisions that the court is able to make during the course of the litigation (or in some cases prior to or upon initial filing of the litigation). These decisions may become permanent or long term depending on how the litigation goes. These requests are made via a submission to the court called a motion (in Hebrew a Bakasha בקשה) literally translated as a request.

Following is a list of some of the typical Motions made during the legal proceedings for divorce and ancillary suits in Israel.

Reconciliation (in Hebrew Shalom Bayit שלום בית) literally, "peace in the home".

Shalom Bayit or reconciliation is an order that the Rabbinic court can give that basically says to the couple: "We are not going to let you proceed in getting divorce right now, go and try to work it out by yourselves". Now sometimes, the court may condition it on your seeing a social worker or a psychologist or a particular Rabbi; but otherwise it is just that they can't continue until they

You can watch a video about these agreements at http://s87.eu/shalom-bayit.

have gone through the period of reconciliation determined by the court.

Use of a Car (or other asset) Order

An order for the use of a car or of other assets is an order that the court will sometimes give when they think that a side is justified in making a request. For example, if a couple is getting divorced and they only have one car and the mother needs the car to take the kids to school or to after school clubs (in Hebrew, Chugim חוגים) then there is a good chance that the court will give the mother an order for the use of the car.

Stop Order (in Hebrew, Tzav Eekoov צו עיקוב) literally, a following order

A Tzav Eekoov is an order that prevents somebody from leaving the country. In other words, a person who has a Tzav Eekoov or a stop order against them will get to the airport and they basically won't be allowed to leave the country and get on the plane. That being said, upon application to the court that granted the order, the person will generally be able to leave if they meet certain terms and conditions that are either written in the stop order or decided by the court. Sometimes the terms will be money issues. For example the court may require the person to put up an amount of security (either in cash or sometimes other assets); sometimes the court will require the party who wants to leave to give the divorce or 'Get' to the other party. But the bottom line is the person cannot leave while there is an open tzav eekoov against them.

> **Did you know?**
> The average Israeli family size is 3.7 people – a number that has not changed in the last 10 years.

Parental Capability Evaluation

An order for a parental capability evaluation (in Hebrew,

Misoogalut Horit *מסוגלות הורית*) is basically an order to have either a social worker or a psychologist make an evaluation of either or both parents capabilities of child rearing. This is important because these evaluations can be the basis for custody and/or visitation orders and even judgements later down the line. It is very important that if this order is given and you are evaluated, that you do not bad mouth your spouse at these meetings. Your focus must be on your child(ren) and what would be best for them without any connection to what your husband says or does, or how he acts. You should emphasize the importance to you that he have a good connection with your child(ren) now, and in the future after you divorce.

Specific housing (in Hebrew Madoor Spatzifee *מדור ספציפי*)

This a special order that a wife can get, which basically prevents the husband from selling the house or from forcing the sale of the house

To see a video on this type of order, visit

http://4ui.us/habitation.

to split the couple's assets while the wife is still living in the house and especially, while she is living in the house with the children.

An order to give information
This order can be given against you by your husband or against a third party or against your husband by you. This order forces those parties who receive the order to provide financial information to the other side or to the other side's attorney so that they can utilize the information for the lawsuit in the division of assets and for the lawsuit in child support.

Rebellious wife
An order for declaring somebody to be a rebellious wife, is an

order that is sometimes given by the Rabbinic court. It may be given in the event that a wife either a) stops having marital relations with her husband; or b) or will make food for the whole family, but not for the husband, or c) won't clean her husband's clothes when she cleans the rest of the family clothes, etc. If that type of order is given by the Rabbinic court, then that woman will not be entitled to get the money that she is entitled to under her Katoova or Jewish writ of marriage.

Dmei Katoova Order

This is an order against the husband to pay to the wife the money specified in the Katoova that the wife is entitled to under their Jewish contract act of marriage. Under this order, which is usually given pursuant to a separate lawsuit, what will

Go to http://4ui.us/dmei-ktoova to see a video on when a woman may get her dmei katoova.

happen is that if the husband has not been meeting his obligations to the wife, (e.g. either he has not treated her properly or he has abused her or he has had an affair) then he will be ordered to pay the sum fixed in the Katoova. In point of fact, this almost never happens, as most divorces end in an agreement at one point or another, and one of the first conditions of divorce agreements is usually the Dmei Katoova is given up.

Restraining orders

There are all sorts of restraining orders that the court can give. The court (either Rabbinic or Family) y can give orders restraining one person from either phoning the other person; being in the house, talking to the other person, getting within 500 meters of one site (like the other side's office and/or the house) etc.. These are orders that are generally given when there is a fear of what is called family violence (in Hebrew Alimoot BaMishpacha *עלימות במשפחה*).

KEDEM MISHPAT. THE PRE-TRIAL CONFERENCE.

No, it's not some new type of grape juice If you are doing any type of litigation in the Family court, you will eventually be given notice of a hearing called the Pre-Trial Conference (in Hebrew, Kedem Mishpat קדם משפט), literally a "pre-trial" hearing. Generally there will be a number of these hearings throughout the litigation period, and in these hearings the idea is not that they are evidentiary hearings (i.e. where testimony is taken and evidence presented) but that the judge is trying to establish a few things for him or herself: timelines with regards to how the trial will continue; whether or not the sides can be pushed and/or bridged into an agreement;

To learn more about the pretrial conference in the Family court you can watch the video at http://s87.eu/pretrial.

who the parties are; and what the real issues between them are. These hearings may also be used by the judge to make interim decisions on motions (some of which were looked at in the previous chapter of this book) that the sides have submitted and responded to in front of him or her.

HOW DO YOU GET INFORMATION AFTER THE DIVORCE LAWSUIT HAS BEEN FILED?

Israel works differently than other countries with regards to the discovery process. The discovery process is the methodology by which the litigants (the parties to a lawsuit) are able to get information from the other side. In other countries the discovery process includes depositions (the taking of parties testimony outside of the courtroom and in front of a stenographer), interrogatories (written questions that must be answered), and requests for admissions (basically interrogatories that say "admit or deny that...."). In Israel these discovery tools generally don't exist in the divorce context.

This is the reason that if you suspect that your husband is hiding assets or other things you should start preparing for your divorce by doing your homework prior to filing. You will find out more information about how to do this later in this book. The other thing that I strongly suggest that you do is to hire a

PI (private detective). Time and again we have found that when women suspect that their husbands are hiding something, they usually are. If it's important to you and you think that assets are being hidden, then the price of the PI will usually pay for itself many times over, and if nothing is found then at least for a few thousand shekels you will gain some peace of mind.

The discovery process in Israeli divorce and family law occurs mainly in two ways. The first way is via the filing of the complaint and answer themselves. There are forms (sort of like case information sheets) that each party has to fill in and when done properly they include and/or reference many documents that are supposed to shed light on the case. They include things like amounts spent, assets owned, etc. If, as I have suggested, you have done your homework and know what the answers to these questions should be, then in the event that your husband lies in filling out the forms, you can make motions to the court to compel him to produce documents. In the event that he doesn't do so, you can ask for the court to issue orders on third parties (banks, partners, accountants, etc.) to give you the information which you are seeking.

> **Did you know?**
> The five main reasons for divorces in Israel are: affairs, no more love, spouses grow apart, disagreements between spouses, and economic problems.

Remember, if you are able to prove to the Family court judge or to the Rabbinic court judges that your husband has hidden assets and has been lying to the court, then the court is likely to find in your favor for the maximum amount that the law allows for in that case (i.e. not always 50-50).

THE SCENARIOS IN WHICH
YOUR DIVORCE CASE WILL END

Most divorces ends in one of two scenarios – either 1) the husband and wife reach a comprehensive divorce agreement , or 2) a Family court Judge and / or Rabbinical court judges or a combination thereof make judicial rulings. There is a third scenario – which is what I call the nightmare scenario – when all of the issues except for the divorce itself are resolved by judicial rulings, but the parties don't get divorced. This leaves one of the parties an "Agun" עגון or an "Agunah" עגונה (m/f) – literally somebody who has been chained. Under Israeli (and Jewish) law, this is a person whose spouse has been unwilling to grant them or accept from them a religious writ of divorce (a Get). This occurs when one of the parties is unwilling to get divorced regardless of what the judges say. This, in the case of a woman, makes it impossible for the chained woman to remarry, and if she has children, they will be categorized under Israeli and Jewish law as "Mamzerim" (and the consequences of this categorization are beyond the scope of this book, but believe me that there is nothing good or beneficial about this categorization). In the case of a man, this

> **Did you know?**
> Six percent of all families in Israel are single parent families with children under the age of 17.

prevents him from getting remarried unless a) if he is Sephardic* he gets a permission from the Rabbinic court to have a second wife, or b) if he is Ashkenazic** he gets 100 Rabbis to essentially annul his marriage and let him take on a second wife.

* a Jew of Middle Eastern or oriental descent   ** a Jew of European descent

DIVORCE VIA A DIVORCE AGREEMENT

Most divorces will end in a divorce agreement – but the real question is how the couple gets there. The divorce agreement can be made at any time – before litigation has started, after litigation has started, in the middle of the litigation itself, and after judgements have been issued by one of the courts, but prior to the giving of the get itself (although I have to stress that couples rarely get into divorce agreements after one side feels they have "won" major battles in litigation). As a practicality, I only recommend to women to reach an agreement after they have begun litigation by filing the relevant lawsuits in the courts which will give them the best deal. Nothing can be as devastating as beginning to work on a divorce agreement with your husband only to find that (maybe because he didn't like the way things were going in the negotiations or maybe because he had planned it all along) he has filed lawsuits for divorce etc. in the courts that are less advantageous to you – and that you are now stuck with those courts.

> **Did you know?**
> The average difference of ages between Jewish men and women for their first marriage is 2.1 years, and for people of other faiths it is 5 years.

In any case, after you have filed, the real question for you should be "How do couples get to comprehensive divorce agreements?" There are a number of manners that are employed to get to comprehensive divorce agreements. Sometimes the **couple is able to agree on all of the issues by themselves**, in which case they go to an attorney and have the terms they agreed to drafted into a formal divorce agreement. <u>I CANNOT EMPHASIZE ENOUGH TO YOU THAT YOU SHOULD NEVER DO THIS. YOU MUST HAVE YOUR OWN ATTORNEY TO AT LEAST REVIEW THE DIVORCE AGREEMENT THAT YOU WILL BE ENTERING INTO. USING THE SAME ATTORNEY WILL ENSURE THAT THERE IS NOBODY TO LOOK AFTER YOUR INTERESTS.</u> In other words, even if you and your husband agree to all of the terms of your divorce and have it drafted by an attorney into a formal divorce agreement, you should go to another attorney who will only be representing you to review and amend the agreement.

Many times the couples are represented by different attorneys and the **attorneys negotiate** for and on behalf of the parties – sometimes with the parties attending and sometimes without their attendance.

Mediation is also a viable alternative to help you reach an agreement. In mediation the couple meets with a mediator – sometimes together, sometimes alone, sometimes with their attorneys – each as determined by the mediator – and the mediator tries to facilitate the couple's reaching agreements. This is usually accomplished in a number of "mediation sessions" each lasting between one and three hours. In my not so humble opinion, even though this can be the best manner by which to reach an agreement, it can also be the most risky. If you ask me, before going to any mediation you must meet with an attorney and learn what your legal rights are and make an outline of the issues and where the law falls, and you must find out what all of your family assets and liabilities are. Without this information, going into

> **Did you know?**
> Forty seven percent of married people believe that their lives will improve in the future compared to fifty four percent of divorced people.

mediation can end up costing you a lot more money and aggravation through the years than you will be saving.

Sometimes a Family court judge may agree to help the couple come to a compromise pursuant to **Section 79A of the Court law**. In this case, rather than having to follow through with the whole litigation process, and in the Family Court judge's discretion, the judge may offer to take into account all of the documents in front of him (the complaints, the answers, and motions, and protocols from any hearings) and issue a binding decision for the couple regarding all of their outstanding issues. I tend to think of this more as **binding arbitration by the Family court judge** rather than going through the full blown litigation. The potential advantages are that it cuts down on the time and emotional toll and sometimes financial toll that long drawn out litigation takes of both sides.

> **Did you know?**
> In November,2012, Tzchian Ping of northern China sued his wife when he found out that her beauty was due to plastic surgery unbeknownst to him, which led to the birth of an ugly daughter. He was awarded seventy five thousand pounds and granted a divorce.

The best thing about getting divorced via an agreement is that there is no limit on how creative you can be. In one case, the couple decided to purchase a small apartment around the corner from where their joint marital home was – rather than selling the home - and each of the "ex-spouses" after the divorce would alternate living in the former marital home. The children stayed in the marital home and the parents moved. Each week one was in the house and the other was in the small apartment and the next week they switched. Now, I am not saying that this is a good idea or even that it is viable for most couples, but I am saying that this is something that no judge or dayan in Israel would ever have arranged for in a judgement – even though it worked for this couple.

In any case, once a divorce agreement has been reached it is executed by the parties and then has to be affirmed as a judgement by a court. If the executed divorce agreement is affirmed as a judgement by the Family court, which takes one court hearing, the Family court judgement will then have to be "affirmed" by the Rabbinic court (one hearing) after which the "Get ceremony" will occur (usually but not always on a different day). In other words – generally there are a total of three court hearings. For the record, this is the method which I highly recommend to most women. This is because even though it is negligibly more expensive, it secures Family court jurisdiction in the event of any future litigation (generally regarding custody/visitation and/or child support issues)

> **Did you know?**
> People who have a feeling of "cold feet" prior to getting married are more likely to get divorced.

In any case, alternatively, if the executed divorce agreement is affirmed as a judgement by the Rabbinic court, which takes one court hearing, you still have to have the "Get ceremony" which will usually occur on a different day – i.e. generally two court hearings.

DIVORCE VIA JUDICIAL RULING (LITIGATION)

This is where you hear of couples "fighting it out in court". Many times a woman will find herself in this type of situation because her spouse will not be willing to resolve their issues in a fair and equitable manner. Here, the issues in front of the Family court will be decided by a single judge who will hear the case, and the issues in front of the Rabbinic court will be decided by three judges. In no case will there ever be a jury. This just doesn't exist in the Israeli system. In this case there will be a trial, which may take several days – not necessarily consecutively, where each side presents their evidence. The judge (or judges in the Rabbinic court) will make decisions about each issue presented before them, and issue judgements. Again, it is important to remember that the Family court will never issue a judgement for divorce, only the Rabbinic court can do that. Generally, the Family court judgements will be on the following broad issues: division of assets, child custody and visitation, and child support. The most important thing for you to do if your divorce case goes this way is to make sure that you and your lawyer are ready for the process. This means that you must work with your lawyer to get him all the information that he requires – these are the "tools" that he will need to be able to present your case. The use and submission of these materials can be very time sensitive and can have a disastrous effect on your case if not submitted in time. This is the reason that I suggest that you prepare carefully before filing for divorce, by following the suggestions that I give in this book for gathering financial and other information before making your first move. It is important to understand that getting divorced via litigation will take more time than any other methodology – almost never less than six months and sometimes going on for years.

> **Did you know?**
> In December 2011, a 99 year old Italian man, Antonio, got divorced from his 96 year old wife of sixty years, Roza, after he found love letters that she wrote to a lover from 1940.

APPEALS

I guess the only saving grace of going through full blown divorce litigation is the fact that if you are unhappy with the outcome, and it is in violation of law, you can appeal. In Family court cases you have a right to appeal to the local District court within 45 days of getting the final judgement, and in Rabbinic court cases you can appeal to the High Rabbinic Appeals court within 30 days of getting the final judgement. Appeals can be very expensive and usually take from a few months up to half a year. Appeals are not usually won, with only a small percentage of lower courts' decisions being overturned.

KNOWING WHAT YOUR RIGHTS ARE

The first thing that most women want to know when they come to see me is what their rights are and what they are entitled to. In order to give them this information, I need to know many facts. The number of years of the marriage, number of children and ages, what real estate and other assets each party has and how and when they were acquired, what debts each party has and how and when it was acquired, what types of insurances the parties have, the incomes of each spouse, etc. Only when I have all of this information am I able to begin to explain to these women what their rights are and what they are legally entitled to.

ALIMONY

One of the things that differentiates Israel the most from other Western countries when it comes to divorce is the issue of alimony. In most Western countries, when there is a disproportionate level of income between spouses (usually because one stayed at home to raise children) then upon divorce it is expected that for a certain time period the spouse who earned less would be entitled to a monthly payment from the other spouse, which is called alimony.

In Israel there is generally no alimony after divorce. As between Jewish spouses in Israel, *for so long as they are married the husband has an obligation to support his wife*. This means that the husband has to pay for clothing, food, household bills, etc. to keep his wife at the lifestyle she was accustomed to. I tell you this because many times women fear that if they sue for divorce their husbands will simply stop depositing their paychecks into the joint pool and will stop paying bills. Legally, the husband cannot unilaterally do this. What this means in practice is that if litigation is taking a long time, there may be room to bring a suit for alimony – but it is important to understand that as soon as the divorce goes through, unless agreed to via a binding divorce agreement, your ex-husband will not be obligated to make any payments to you above and beyond those that he is required to make for child support.

There is an exception to the above called rehabilitative alimony – whereby the court occasionally (but very rarely) will award a woman who has stayed at home so that her husband could build his career a small alimony payment for a short defined period (almost never exceeding 2-3 years) so that the wife can acclimate herself to and find work.

To see videos about alimony in Israel go to http://4ui.us/alimony1 or http://4ui.us/alimony2.

The bottom line is that you should not bank on getting alimony from your husband after the divorce goes through. You should work with you legal representative to help you to do the calculations on what you will get from the division of assets and what you should expect from child support in order to be able to calculate how you will be able to afford your living expenses after the divorce.

CUSTODY / VISITATION

Custody in Israel is separate and apart from guardianship. Usually one parent will have custody but both parents will have guardianship (in Hebrew, Aptroposoot אפוטרופוסות) over the minor children. As a practical matter what this means is that both parents are considered legally responsible for the child, and that both parents are entitled to have a say regarding education, health care, etc. If the parents cannot agree then the issue will be decided (on an ongoing basis) by a court. Generally, the issue at hand in divorce litigation is not guardianship, but physical custody over the minor children – i.e. where will they be spending most of their time.

No matter which court hears your custody case (i.e. the Family court or the Rabbinic court), the standard that is supposed to be utilized is what is known as "the best interests of the child." What this means is that the court is supposed to make an evaluation as to which parent it will be in the best interests of the child to live with. The way that the court does this is by making an evaluation of the family and determining who the main caregiver for the child or children should be. The courts will generally appoint a social worker and/or a psychologist to do an evaluation regarding this issue – it is often said that the social worker or psychologist acts as the eyes of the court. The social worker and/or psychologist evaluation will generally include visits or meetings with the children, with each parent, and/or with each parent and the children. They will also generally speak with children's teachers – especially if the children are younger. The court will get the report (evaluation) and will utilize it in rendering custody and visitation decisions. Many times the judge (or dayanim) will "rubber stamp" the recommendations of the report, so I cannot emphasize enough how important these reports are and how you must try to work in conjunction with the social worker or psychologist. You will find that these reports almost never recommend on splitting up children – and usually if one parent is the best caregiver in the best interests of the child evaluation, they will have custody for all minor children.

Additionally, Israel employs something called "the tender age doctrine." This doctrine says that there is a presumption (which is overcome able) that the best interests of children under the age of six is to be under the custody of their mother.

All this being said, in the vast majority of cases in Israel, custody over minor children goes to the mother. The general visitation schedules in Israel are twice a week for the non-custodial parent (usually the father), with or without sleepovers, plus alternate weekends.

You can see a video on typical visitation arrangements at http://4ui.us/visitation.

Vacation periods and holidays are generally divided equally between both parents on an alternate basis.

Finally, I have to address the issue of joint custody. First of all, if you and your husband come to an agreement that you will both have joint custody (i.e. that the children will spend an equal amount of time with each parent) then the courts will generally go along with your agreement. Whether the agreement be that the kids are with one parent from Sunday to

Tuesday and the other parent from Wednesday to Friday and alternate Shabbatot (Saturdays) or whether the kids alternate between each parent each night, the courts will generally accept such an agreement.

However, what we find is that more and more fathers are suing for joint custody over their children. For the most part, the courts are not awarding joint custody, and in many cases even see it for what it sometimes is – an attempt by the father to make an argument for lower child support (in Hebrew Mezonot מזונות) payments. However, the pendulum is changing on this issue, and if your husband has been the main caregiver for your children, then beware that he may attempt to get joint custody.

> Watch a video about joint custody in Israel by going to http://s87.eu/joint-custody.

RULES ABOUT THE COURT ORDERED EVALUATION

Before you meet with the psychologist or social worker that the court appoints for your case, there are some general rules which you must follow if you want the report to reflect positive on you.

1. Unless you feel that your Hebrew is perfect, you should ask to speak to the evaluator in English. I cannot tell you how many times we have had clients "mess up" by using the wrong word or improperly conjugating a word and having the evaluator understand the exact opposite of what they were trying to say.

2. Don't refer to your kids as "my child" or "my children" but as "our child" or "our children".

3. Never speak badly about your spouse in front of your children.

4. You and your husband probably don't agree with each other regarding your philosophies regarding raising the children. The court won't choose one parenting style over the other per say. However, rather than fighting with your husband about it, try to find a mutually acceptable children's therapist to mediate during the course of the divorce.

5. If you think that there is going to be a legal custody battle, talk to a lawyer experienced in contested custody cases to learn what you should or should not be doing.

6. One of the single biggest factors that will make a judge consider granting a father custody or lowering child support payments is if the father does not have access or has very restricted access to his child. Do not fall into the trap of punishing your spouse by limiting his visits with your joint children.

   To see a video explaining why a psychologist may be involved in your divorce case, go to http://4ui.us/psychologist.

7. Introducing new partners into your child's life before you are divorced is considered damaging to the child. Don't introduce a boyfriend or a girlfriend before the divorce is finalized, and even after that I would suggest that you do so in coordination with consultation with a child's psychologist.

CHILD SUPPORT

The next issue is computing what you should expect for child support (in Hebrew, Mezonot Yeladim מזונות ילדים). Israeli law regarding child support in marriages between Jews, goes in accordance with Jewish law. What that means is that the sole responsibility for raising the child (financially anyway) is upon the father - at least until age 16. Then after the age of 16, in very few limited cases, in accordance with Jewish law regarding of charity, if the wife is rich and the husband is poor then the expense may be shared. But the bottom line is that the base law, which applies to the vast majority of Jewish marriages in Israel, is that the father bears the sole responsibility for raising or rather for supporting minor children. So, what should you expect to get for child support under Israeli law?

Did you know?
According to a University of Cincinnati study in 2012, married women drink 9 alcoholic beverage on average a month as opposed to 6.5 alcoholic beverages a month drunk by divorced women. However, married men drink an average of 19 alcoholic beverages a month as opposed to 22 alcoholic beverages a month drunk by divorced women.

Well, there are three components that make up the monthly child support payment under Israeli law. The way it works is this: for each child there is a "base" component which is between 1,250 and 1,550 N.I.S per month. This is called Base Support (in Hebrew Mezonot basees בסיס מזונות). That is to cover food, clothing, i.e. "basic" needs.

Then there is a second component which is called the a housing expense (in Hebrew, Madoor מדור). This is set as a percentage of housing costs. For example, with one child it would be 30%; 2 children 40%; 3 children 50% of the housing expense. The housing expense can be either the mortgage or rent and it will also be property taxes (in Hebrew, Arnona ארנונה) electricity, gas, water etc.

The third and last component of child support is a part that gets split between the parents and that is miscellaneous expenses. Those would be health care expenses, school expenses, babysitting for the afternoon expenses, etc. .

The court will usually split the third component between the parents in accordance with their salaries, so that if the husband makes a lot more than the wife; then he will have to pay a lot more than 50% of those expenses. If he makes a lot less than the wife, he may only have to pay 50% or in some cases less than 50% of those expenses.

One of the important things to take into consideration when making these calculations is that when you have multiple children, the "base" component of the child support payment will go down. By way of illustration, let's say that you have 5 children. The "base" child support component of 1,250 to 1,550 NIS per month will usually be lowered for each successive child. Generally it will not be the case that if you have 5 children that the first base component of the child support is going to 7500 shekels. That part would probably be lowered, again, depending on what people are earning.

The big picture is that even if the father is not making any money he will still have to pay these amounts. Why? Because it is his obligation under Jewish law. Thereby under Israeli law, these are his obligations towards his children, and of course this amount is going to be paid to the custodial parent - and that is generally the wife.

The other part of the big picture is that the father really almost never pays enough – but as I always tell my divorce clients (both male and female) – if you were struggling financially before divorce, please understand that you will be struggling financially even more (at least initially) after divorce. And why is this? Because supporting two separate households statistically costs 135% of the original expenses that a couple has when married.

You can see a video on computing how much child support to expect by going to http://4ui.us/child-support.

FIGURING OUT HOW YOUR ASSETS
AND DEBTS WILL BE DIVIDED

The general rule in Israel is that assets and debts which were acquired during the course of marriage, are going to be split equally at the time of divorce. What that means is that anything that you brought while you were together is going to be split between the two of you. On the other hand, any debts that you have built up while you were together are going to be split as well. This includes pensions. It includes real estate owned, stock accounts, cars and so on. It also includes credit card debt, mortgages, bank loans, etc. There are some exceptions to this rule, which I will address below.

Regarding things that were acquired before the marriage, that's a more interesting question. If there were things that were kept totally separate they will remain the property of the spouse who owned it prior to the marriage. For example, if you have an apartment that you rent out, that you owned before you were married, and you did not use that rent money to run your household and did not put that rent money into a joint bank account, and you did not live in the apartment while married, then that apartment will remain yours generally. Of course the same is true if that apartment was his prior to marriage and he had kept it separate. In short: things that were acquired before the marriage and kept totally separate will remain the separate property of the spouse who owned them before marriage. Things that were commingled will be split equally. So, as another example, if your husband inherited $200,000.00 from one of his parents and you used that money to put an addition on the house, well your husband has his lost. Or if you used that money and you put it together with other money that you had and bought another house that you are renting out, then your husband has lost it. You should expect to get half of that.

It's very important to try to figure out, before you filing your divorce papers, exactly what you can expect to receive and what you can expect to have to transfer over to your husband. Of course, there are also other exceptions to the rules that I stated above. For example, if you had a prenuptial agreement, you are going to go in accordance with *You can see a video on how assets get divided during divorce in Israel by going to http://s87.eu/assets.* whatever the prenuptial agreement said. So to summarize regarding inheritances: if you inherited money that was kept totally separate while you were married then it will continue to be totally yours after you divorce. If you commingled it then it will be split.

But again, this is the type of thing that you really should come into my office and discuss. When I work with my clients we generally look at each asset and try to figure out who will end up with which asset in the event of litigation. Generally we will have a pretty good idea of what it is that you can expect to keep or get out during divorce – in ordinary situations.

THE LOW DOWN ON "SHALOM BAYIT" – AGREEMENT OR COURT ORDERED RECONCILIATION

In the divorce process in Israel, when we talk about Shalom Bayit שלום בית or "reconciliation", we are really talking about two different things. The first one is an agreement. A lot of times a couple will start down the road towards divorce and then at a certain point realize for whatever reason that they still want to stay with each other. Maybe it's because they still love each other. Maybe it's for the kids. Maybe it's because of financial issues. But the bottom line is that they want to keep trying, but they want to change things. In that case, they can reach a reconciliation agreement. By the way, I don't let my clients sign a reconciliation agreement unless it's a two part agreement. It's a reconciliation agreement in the alternative divorce agreement. This is called a Heskem Shalom Bayit viLeChilufin Gerushin הסכם שלום בית ולחילופין גירושין in Hebrew. I do this so that if the reconciliation does not work, we all know the terms of how the couple will get divorced and we don't end up back in the great mystery tour. In any case; that's the first usage in family law in Israel in Shalom Bayit of reconciliation.

You can watch a video about shalom bayit agreements at http://s87.eu/shalom-bayit.

The second one and the more devious one, is court ordered reconciliation which is generally in the Rabbinic court. What happens is one of the spouses generally uses it as a tactic. The spouse makes a motion for Shalom Bayit (reconciliation) and if the court decides "yes we are ordering Shalom Bayit", then they are essentially ordering reconciliation and they will give a period, let's say 90 days - during which time they won't let the couple get divorced. If one person wants the other person out of the house, and the other person either won't leave or has an order that they are supposed to do Shalom Bayit or reconciliation and therefore they can't be forced out in any case, then the side that did not want the order is going to be pressured to reach an agreement. An agreement reached during this period may not be as good as an agreement otherwise negotiated – because of the pressure of being forced to live together to try to reconcile. So, it's really turned into a tactical thing where you basically ask the court (and again it's generally the Rabbinic court) to order a period of reconciliation during which you are not going to able to move forward in your divorce. This adds to pressure in the household which is really

You can watch a video on shalom bayit motions at http://4ui.us/shalom-lawsuit.

not a good thing – especially during the period while you are getting divorced - and generally it's not a tactic that I would use.

Don't misunderstand - I'm all for reconciliation and a lot of times I will turn clients away and tell them "Until you have gone for some couples counselling, I would rather not represent you, because I don't think you are ready for it." But, knowing that ten to fifteen percent of the people who start down the divorce path will end up getting back together, I always try to keep in mind the old saying amongst family law attorneys in Israel. "A couple that has brought suits to get divorced may end up reaching shalom bayit (reconciliation). A couple where one party has sued for shalom bayit will always get divorced."

WHAT HAPPENS IF YOU WANT TO PERMANENTLY LEAVE ISRAEL WITH YOUR CHILDREN DURING OR AFTER THE DIVORCE?

Generally you won't be allowed to permanently leave Israel during your divorce. If you want to make a visit outside of Israel you may be able to, although you will generally have to deposit some type of guarantee with the court to ensure that you and your children will return (and the amount can be hefty – I generally ask the courts not to let children leave during the divorce process unless at least 250,000 NIS is put up as assurance that they will return). However, you generally won't be able to leave Israel during the course of the divorce if it is for purposes of relocation. This is especially true when you have minor children and you want to take them with you.

What about after the divorce? In the typical scenario, the couple has divorced and are living separately; the father has visitation with the kids twice a week and alternate weekends or whatever other agreement the couple has come to. If this is your situation and you decide that you want to leave Israel, are you able to do so, how do you do it?

The answer is that it depends on your factual circumstances, because what happens is that you would have to make a motion to the court (i.e. the one that made the decisions regarding child custody) from your original divorce litigation or the court that entered your divorce agreement. As part of the process, you would make a motion and the court is supposed to look at three things really. The first thing is what type of support network exists for you and or the children in Israel, including a new love interest that you may have outside of Israel; the second thing is financial issues – i.e. if you and the children are living in poverty in Israel and you have a great job offer and/or a proposal to marry a wealthy person outside of Israel this will be taken into consideration; and the third thing is what's in the best interest of the children (in Hebrew tovat hayeledim טובת הילדים).

To see a video addressing leaving Israel with children after divorce, go to http://4ui.us/leave-Israel.

There are a lot of times where the courts will let the custodial ex-spouse (i.e. generally the ex-wife) leave the country with the children. However, even in the cases where they do allow the ex-spouse to leave, the courts are really careful about making sure that there are mechanisms in place so that the parent who is left behind in Israel has a regular connection with his or her children. As an example, a classic case would be a mother of three who has no family here in Israel, does not speak Hebrew well, has special needs children, and is living below the poverty level but meets a wealthy man who happens to live next to her parents, outside of Israel, and wants to get married and live in her original home country, where there is very good and specialized care for her special needs children. I would say that in that type of case there would be a high chance of success that the woman would be allowed to leave.

But again what's really important is that you just don't pick up and go. If you pick up and leave without getting a court order allowing you to do so first, then that is considered kidnapping under the Hague Convention. Generally when taken to countries that are members of the Hague convention (i.e. most western countries), the children may forcibly be returned and in that case you will probably lose custody if you are the custodial parent.

QUESTIONS THAT YOU HAVE TO CONSIDER BEFORE HIRING A DIVORCE ATTORNEY

For most people, choosing a divorce lawyer is a daunting task. You are about to embark on an unfamiliar and treacherous journey through the legal system. To make things worse you have to do this while you are in the grip of extreme emotional turmoil. Guiding you through this dramatic life experience should be a lawyer that you can trust completely and with whom you can establish a close working relationship which will continue for as long as you need. For weeks, months, and in rare cases even for years. Throughout this selection process remind yourself that all lawyers are not created equal. Protect yourself by carefully considering the following questions before making payment arrangements:

> **Did you know?**
> The percentage of working men who get divorced is lower than the percentage of unemployed men or men working in non-permanent positions that get divorced.

1. Is the lawyers practice focus exclusively on family law? You should choose a lawyer who exclusively or at least primarily practices in the area of matrimonial and family law. This is a constantly evolving, highly complex area of practice, and you need in your corner a knowledgeable

61

and experienced lawyer who is intimately familiar with the intricacies of divorce law and family matters. You cannot leave the welfare of your children or your future financial security, in the hands of a "jack of all trades, master of none" attorney.

2. Is the lawyer attentive when you are talking? It's crucial to have an initial face to face consultation with any potential lawyer before signing a written payment agreement. An initial consultation is a golden opportunity to assess whether the attorney will treat you with compassion and dedication or whether you are just going to be another number in a book and a faceless file stuck in a corner in his office. If the lawyer is checking his emails, typing away, and on his telephone or taking other calls during your meeting, you really should think about going elsewhere.

3. Does the lawyer have an office policy insuring the timely return of phone calls? Communication between attorney and client is a key in any divorce action. A lawyer should be reachable by phone and email. Unfortunately, clients' main complaints against divorce lawyers are that the lawyers fail to respond in a timely manner to emails, telephone calls or other communications. Ask any lawyer you consider retaining whether there is an office policy regarding the prompt return of phone calls and emails. If he hesitates, there likely is no such policy and you will be frustrated to no end in trying to get in touch with him or her.

Did you know?
In 2015 Tel Aviv was the city with the greatest number of divorces in Israel, a title held by Jerusalem until 2014.

4. Is the lawyer selective in accepting cases? Does the lawyer you are considering accept every client that walks through the door? Or does his or her practice consist of fewer, but select clients? In order to provide dedicated and comprehensive service an attorney owes it to existing clients to be highly selective and accepting new matters, make sure that this is the case with your attorney.

5. Is your personality compatible with your lawyer's personality? In order to work effectively with your lawyer, you have to be comfortable with him or her. Make sure that the lawyer you are retaining is someone that you can talk to, that you can listen to, and that you will be able to share the most intimate details of your life and finances without feeling threatened in any way.

6. Does the lawyer treat you with compassion and empathy? Make sure the lawyer treats you as the unique individual that you are. A good lawyer will be eager to listen to your marital history and will make sure to fully understand your priorities and your objectives without being in a rush to simply categorize you and hurry you out the door.

7. Is the lawyer proactive? You should hire a divorce lawyer who is able to provide you with a plan of action. This attorney should listen to you and then take charge.

8. Will the lawyer be involved in your case personally? If your case is also handled by an associate or paralegal when will your attorney be involved? You do not want to go to a firm where you meet the attorney at the initial

meeting and then never see them again. While it is understandable that in successful law practices there is the lead attorney on a case and then associates doing the legal "grunt work", you must be satisfied that any staff member working, on your case is competent and experienced. You must know when and how you will be in contact with the lead attorney, even though you may be in contact with the associate attorney for much of the day to day interaction. This is essential.

9. Is the lawyer willing to attempt and negotiate settlement on your matter? Only a very small percentage of divorce cases actually go to trial. The vast majority of cases are settled, some on the court house steps on the very day of trial. A good attorney knows that there is no court winner in a divorce or custody trial. If it's left unchecked, the process can be emotionally and financially devastating to both sides. Your attorney should therefore make every reasonable effort to negotiate a settlement on your behalf - while at the same time diligently prepare your case for the potentiality of the trial. Cases are settled when the lawyers are both prepared and dedicated.

> **Did you know?**
> Seventy percent of divorces in Israel are initiated by women.

10. Is the lawyer willing to educate you and to answer your questions? Your divorce lawyer must be a good communicator and be willing to answer all your questions. Any skilled divorce lawyer knows that educated clients are better equipped to make good and informed decisions with regard to their and their family's future.

11. Is the lawyer assertive without being arrogant? Many people make the mistake of looking for divorce lawyer that will be "pit-bull". In hiring a divorce lawyer remember that louder, does not necessarily mean better. A good attorney will not feel the need to compensate for a lack of skill by being obnoxious. A good attorney will aggressively and effectively advocate for you, but without an ego that squeezes the air out of any room.

12. Is the lawyer being honest with you? Or are you being promised the sun, the moon and the stars? Be very weary of any lawyer who guarantees a specific result in your divorce case. All litigation is risky and can be influenced by present circumstances, future developments and the decisions and the attitude of the judge. Every case has strengths and weaknesses and your lawyer should be able to point out both. You can trust an attorney who tells it like it is, and who is candid with you about your chances of getting a particular outcome. You can't trust an attorney who simply tells you what you want to hear.

13. Does a lawyer underscore that your children's best interests are your highest priorities? No parent should ever use his children as pawns in a divorce action. Your children's welfare and best interest should be your paramount priority. Any good lawyer will understand and support this objective and will caution you that manipulating your children will be devastating to them personally.

> **Did you know?**
> For first time marriages, the older a woman is on her wedding day the lower the chance that she will divorce.

14. Does the lawyer present himself or herself well? If you

are put off by the lawyer personal grooming and dress, behavior, or language, then chances are that the judge and the opposing counsel may be also. If a lawyer's office is a mess of dirty pizza boxes, dirty clothes, and legal documents that he or she prepares on your behalf; it is likely to reflect that the work product on your case, will not be thoughtful, cogent and organized either. You want an attorney who cares enough to present him or herself, the staff, and the office in a professional manner.

15. Is the lawyer able to utilize the latest technology? In this day and age your lawyer should be up to date on the latest technological developments. Your lawyer should understand how computers, the internet are changing communications, relationships and society. If a lawyer has chosen to remain blindly old school about technology, do you think he or she cares enough to stay up to date with the latest developments in the law?

16. Does your lawyer speak your language and understand the mentality and culture you are coming from? Here in Israel, I would not call ourselves a melting pot like in the U.S., but I would call us a salad. We have different groups of people that stay mainly in the same ethnic and or social types of groups that they stayed in their home countries. This is because such a large number of us are immigrants who have moved here from other countries. You really have to make sure that your attorney has an understanding of where you are at. Not only in terms of language, also in terms of mentality. If you need to hire a divorce lawyer, you really have to be sure to do your homework and to consider these questions before signing a retainer agreement.

The last thing you need during your divorce case is to waste your precious energy, money and disagreement with your lawyer. So, be sure to hire the right lawyer from the start and save yourself the agony of lost time, big bills and endless frustration.

STEPS YOU SHOULD BE TAKING TO PREPARE FOR A POSSIBLE DIVORCE

Some people say that you should take as much time to plan your divorce as you did to plan your wedding. Here are some steps that every woman should be taking in order to prepare for divorce.

First of all, you should consult an attorney about your legal rights. This is very important, because different situations can lead to different legal rights and you have to know what it is that you can expect. Secondly, you should write a narrative for the attorney, detailing the date that you got married or if you lived together before getting married, the ~~that~~ date you started living together, children's birthdates, if you ever separated, or what assets you acquired and what separate property each of you brought into the marriage. My office gives all of our potential clients a diary to write all this information. You should gather information about what you own and what you owe; copies of financial statements, tax returns, and retirement plan documents, brokerage statements, insurance

> **Did you know?**
> The percentage of divorces amongst couples with academic degrees is lower than that amongst couples with no academic degrees.

policies. You should also get detailed information about each retirement plan, in which either you and or your husband has participated.

You should think about what assets you would like to keep if you get divorced and what you are willing to give up. You might even consult with your accountant about the tax consequences of various options, especially if you have overseas assets in your original home country or any third party countries. You should get preliminary estimates of the value of the property you own and you should list all of the debts that you owe. You should also try to pay bills and credit card from joint funds before you get divorce, so that you don't get stuck with them later. You should find out what is in the safety deposit box, if there is one, and you should get both keys if possible.

You should get a spending history. Prepare a spending history for the last year from your checkbooks so that you can get a real good idea of your future needs, and decide where to cut back as necessary, and to have it to fill out paperwork for child support motions. Also you should use your joint funds to repair your automobile, your home, to buy clothes for you and your children, and to get dental work done. If you

> **Did you know?**
> Statistically, there is a large increase in divorce proceedings initiated after the holidays in the Jewish month of Tishrei and Nissan.

wait until after the divorce, these are going to be your expenses to bear alone. You should also set aside cash reserves to use for the first few months of your divorce process. Practically what this means is that you should transfer your share and only your share of the joint funds to your separate bank account and you should do that immediately before filing.

You should apply for some credit cards and banks accounts in your own name and in a different bank (not different branch, a different bank) and you should make sure to remember that after the process starts you should close or freeze your joint credit card accounts. You should, if possible, get control over both credit cards on your joint accounts. After filing, you should spate all accounts or alternatively you should notify all the creditors that you are not going to be responsible for your husband's charges on those accounts. You should also open up post office box that you can use for your mail, while you are preparing for and are in the process of divorce, that's private.

You should begin a divorce notebook where you list all the problems with the impending divorce and you should also list each step that you take in the divorce process including a synopsis of telephone calls, conferences with your attorney, accountant, social workers, psychologists, etc. and keep notes.

The bottom line is that divorce is scary - but it is going to be less so - if you figure out the worst that could happen and decide in advance how you are going to deal with it. In short, you should also explore your career options. Use the crisis of the divorce to put yourself into a more satisfying work position. You should also begin negotiation discussions with your husband as calmly as possible. Find out what his hot buttons are and where he is willing to make concessions. I recommend that you find a good therapist or at least a support group to help you go through the months ahead, because divorce is too dramatic to go through alone for most people. Most importantly, take your time and

Did you know?
There are no statistical differences in expected life spans between single people, married people or divorced people except for the ages of 40-59 – during which ages divorced people have a higher expected life span than the other two groups.

don't rush matters, planning for divorce is best done when it's done deliberately and slowly.

When things look grey and downcast - remember - this is your chance for a new start.

FINANCIAL RECORDS THAT EVERY WOMAN NEEDS TO ACQUAINT HERSELF WITH

It constantly amazes me, how women, who are intelligent, educated women, are not familiar with the financial records that affect their everyday lives. If this was you in the past, I am going to help you to make sure that this is not you in the future. So, I'm giving you a list here of financial records which you really should become familiar with, before you start the divorce process.

First of all, if you have a net worth statement, you should make yourself familiar with it or even prepare it if you can. You should get copies of all notes that were signed by you and your husband any mortgages etc. Also if any guarantees (in Hebrew aravoot עֲרֵבוּת) were signed by you or your spouse, get copies of them. You should try and get your U.S tax returns for the last 3 years and your and your husband's Israeli Form 106s for the same periods.

72

You should get the benefits statements from your employer and your spouse's employer for pension plans and profit sharing. You should find your life insurance policies on you and your spouse and on your children. You should find any disability policies that you or your spouse have, both long term and short term. You should get a copy of your home owners' insurance policy, your car insurance policies, and of all health insurance policies. Any long term care insurance policy and really any insurance policies. If you have credit life insurance, if you have mortgage payment insurance, if you have any cancer policies and so on. If you don't know where to start – look at your bank and credit card statements and start calling the companies that are making monthly charges. Which by the way leads me to the suggestion that you should also get copies of all your bank account statements for at least a year, of all the credit card statements for at least a year, and of all your brokerage statements for at least a year - both for joint accounts and accounts held in the name of either you or your spouse. You should make an inventory of personal property and write it down and if possible take pictures. You should get any employment contracts that you or your husband might have, any partnership agreements.

You should find out what the inventory of your lock boxes or your husband's lock box and write it down. If there are any powers of attorney out there for you or your spouse, you should get copies of them. You should take care of your will. Remember: first of all, you should get copies of any wills or trust that you are a beneficiary of; second of all you should make sure that your own personal will is updated as of the date that you started the divorce process, so that it takes in account your new or changing relationship with your spouse.

> **Did you know?**
> People who own their own apartments are 22% less likely to divorce.

If you have any prenuptial agreements you should get those in place. Get copies of any lease agreements or real estate contracts. If you have stocks, any mutual funds statements, and any annuity statements. All of these are documents that you really need to have in order to make the divorce process move much more quickly and smoothly, and to lower the likelihood that your husband or his attorney will try to prevent you from getting what you are legally entitled to.

Of course if you need any help with any of these issues, you should be able to approach your attorney for assistance.

STAGES OF DIVORCE

I am not a psychologist, but after having spoken with many while working on my client's cases, and after I and my staff having been there to support our clients time after time, I have come to understand that divorce is known to be one of the most stressful events that a person may go through in the course of his or her lifetime. Psychologists have noted that during divorce people move through a natural progression in what they call the "stages of divorce." Apparently, every person experiences these stages differently and some people may skip some of the stages. However, since divorce has it's root in marriage, the stages we will look at start to occur during the marriage.

Stage One: Disillusionment
Disillusionment begins when spouses begin to realize that there are some real differences between them. In this stage, a spouse starts to feel that the person who they expect to fulfill almost all of their expectations, needs, and ideals turns out to be: depressed, sloppy, boring, unaffectionate, anti-social, uncaring, insensitive, or anything else that is

Did you know?
Generally, married people are content with their lives in higher ratios than single people and divorced people.

not what they expected when they got married. When people feel these things, it intrudes on the happiness of the marriage, and prolonged time spent dwelling on these feelings sows the seeds of destruction, which leads to stage two.

Stage Two: Erosion

This state is characterized by chipping away of each other's ego. One or the other says, sometimes to his or her self, and sometimes to the other spouse "I'm not getting enough out of this marriage." Sometimes a careful vigilance is maintained by either or both spouses to make sure that one does not give any more than the other. The concentration in this period is on taking rather than giving, being loved instead of loving. Sex becomes a battleground, where fidgety or impotency expresses the frozen anger that exists beneath the surface of the spousal relationship.

Stage Three: Detachment

In the detachment stage the couple no longer cares enough about each other to hate or to fight. Each feels a low commitment to the relationship. They barely talk. They avoid physical affection or sex. They don't look into each other's eyes. This period is not so much of an intensified conflict as it is increasing boredom with the conflict. The coldness that was at first withholding of love has become habitual and natural, empty shells of people pass each other in routine. The detached person begins to dream of his or her own future without the spouse.

Stage four: Physical Separation

For those who have spent a long time preparing to get divorced by building up the courage to leave an entire marriage, the physical separation can be enormous relief. For those who are unprepared and still emotionally involved in the spouse, physical separation can leave a person in shock. But almost all newly separated persons have to face the loneliness, the anxiety, initial confusion and fears. This separation may not be to separate homes – yet – but just may be when one spouse leaves the marital bedroom and just sleeps somewhere else.

Stage Five: Mourning

Mourning is a web of anger, hurt, loneliness, relief and helplessness. Mourning helps a spouse to rid himself or herself of the ghost of the former spouse.

A person says, "I can't go back, but I can't go forward." They want intimacy, but they can't handle it. In this stage the divorcing person moves from no goals to concrete goals. They will take off the

Did you know?
The chance that a couple will divorce goes down by ten percent for each year of marriage.

wedding ring, rearrange the furniture and clean out the old house and begin as a single person. Mourning during divorce enables the releasement of anger. Releasing anger is a necessary part of divorce. Depression may also accompany mourning.

Stage Six: Second Adolescence

Instead of looking back at the former spouse with anger and attraction, the person during the stage is concentrating on his or her personal growth. Choices begin to increase. Vision clears. The excitement of possible new adventures and new risks creates what psychologists perceive to be an almost adolescent state. Previous areas of deprivation, whether sexual, travel, fun, hobbies, friends or training, are often vigorously pursued. Dating often renews all the feelings that people felt when they were adolescent. Is he or she going to call? Will he or she accept the invitation? Are my social skills okay according to today's standards? The divorcing person may feel considerable intrigue and excitement during this stage.

Stage Seven: Exploration and Hard Work

With renewed vitality the divorced individual begins earnestly to pursue self-chosen goals. Instead of seeing overwhelming, unreachable, future aspirations, a plan of action toward manageable, reachable goals has been implemented. New relationships are formed, old ones and relationships with children are enhanced, and you may feel new confidence, a sense of being master over your life. This is what I hope that you get to as quickly as possible.

ENGLISH LANGUAGE BOOKS FOR CHILDREN ON DIVORCE – BY AGE

AGES 3 TO 8

A Day With Daddy by Nikki Grimes (2004). Scholastic. ISBN: 978-0439568500

At Daddy's on Saturdays by Linda Walvoord Girard (1999). Albert Whitman & Company. ISBN: 978-0807504734

Bessie Bump Gets a New Family by Amberley Meredith (2010). Eloquent Books. ISBN: 978- 1609119010

Charlie Anderson by Barbara Abercombie (1995). Margaret K. McElderry Books. ISBN: 978- 0689801143

Dinosaurs Divorce: A Guide for Changing Families by Marc Brown & Laurie Krasny Brown (1999). Brown Books for Young Readers. ISBN: 978-0316109963

Do I Have A Daddy?: A Story About A Single-Parent Child by Jeanne Warren Lindsay (2000). Morning Glory Press. ISBN: 978-0930934446

Good-Bye, Daddy! by Brigitte Weninger (1997). North-South Books. ISBN: 978-1558583832

It's Not Your Fault, Koko Bear: A Read-Together Book for Parents & Young Children During Divorce by Vicki Lansky (1998). Book Peddlers. ISBN: 978-0916773472

Let's Talk About Divorce by Fred Rogers (1996). Puffin. ISBN: 978-0698116702

Loon Summer by Barbara Santucci (2010). Eerdmans Books for Young Readers. ISBN: 978- 0802853899

Mom and Dad Don't Live Together Any More by Kathy Stinson (1988). Tandem Library. ISBN: 978-0785798958

My Family's Changing by Pat Thomas (1999). Barron's Educational Series. ISBN: 978- 0764109959

My Mother's House, My Father's House by C. B. Christiansen (1989). Atheneum. ISBN: 978- 0689313943

Priscilla Twice by Judith Caseley (1995). Greenwillow Books. ISBN: 978-0688133054

Two Homes by Claire Masurel (2003). Candlewick. ISBN: 978-0763619848

Was It the Chocolate Pudding? A Story for Little Kids About Divorce by Sandra Levins & Bryan Langdo (2005). Magination Press. ISBN: 978-1591473091

When My Parents Forgot to Be Friends by Jennifer Moore-Mallinos (2005). Barron's Educational Series. ISBN: 978-0764131721

AGES 6 TO 9

Always My Dad by Sharon Dennis Wyeth (1998). Scholastic. ISBN: 978-0590031738

I Love My Parents, But I Hate Divorce by Pat H. Otto (1997). Wildwater Publications. ISBN: 978- 0965785419

AGES 9 TO 12

Amber Brown Goes Forth by Paula Danziger (1997). Puffin. ISBN: 978-0142409015

Amber Brown Sees Red by Paula Danziger (2009). Puffin. ISBN: 978-0142412619

Blue Sky, Butterfly by Jean van Leeuwen (1996). Dial. ISBN: 978-0803719729

But...What About Me? (How It Feels To Be A Kid In Divorce) by Bonnie Doss & Jennifer Schroeder. (1998). Bookmark Publishers. ISBN: 978-0965389563

Chevrolet Saturdays by Candy Dawson-Boyd (1993). Simon & Schuster Children's Publishing. ISBN: 978-0027117653

Divorce by Debra Goldentyer (1998). Raintree-Steck Vaughn Publishers. ISBN: 978-0817250300

Divorce Is Not the End of the World by Zoe Stern & Evan Stern (2008). Tricycle Press. ISBN: 978- 1582462417

Family Break-Up by Kelly Bishop & Penny Tripp (2003). Heineman Library. ISBN: 978- 0431098104

Ginny Morris and Mom's House, Dad's House by Mary Gallagher (2005). Magination Press. ISBN: 978-1591471578

It's Not the End of the World by Judy Blume (2014). Atheneum. ISBN: 978-1481411165

My Parents Are Divorced, Too: A Book For Kids By Kids by Melanie Ford (2006). Magination Press. ISBN: 978-1591472421

My Parents Are Getting Divorced: How to Keep It Together When Your Mom and Dad Are Splitting Up by Florence Cadier & Melissa Daly. Amulet Books. ISBN: 978-0810991637

My Parents Still Love Me Even Though They're Getting Divorced (an interactive tale for children) by Lois V. Nightingale (1997). Nightingale Rose Publications. ISBN: 978-1889755007

The Squeaky Wheel by Robert Kimmel Smith (2008). iUniverse. ISBN: 978-0595522033

The Trouble with Thirteen by Betty Miles (1984). Avon Books. ISBN: 978-0380674701

What Can I Do? A Book for Children of Divorce by Danielle Lowry (2002). Magination Press. ISBN: 978-1557987709

What Children Need to Know When Parents Get Divorced by William Coleman (1998). Bethany House Publishers. ISBN: 978-0764220517

What Do We Think About: Family Break-Up by Jullian Powell (2001). Hodder Wayland. ISBN: 978-0750232517

Young Adults

For Better, For Worse: A Guide to Surviving Divorce for Preteens and Their Families by Janet Bode (2001). Simon & Schuster Children's Publishing. ISBN: 978-0689819452

I Want Answers and a Parachute by P.J. Petersen (1993). Simon & Schuster Children's Publishing. ISBN: 978-0671865771

Help!: A Girl's Guide to Divorce and Stepfamilies by Nancy Holyoke (1999). American Girl. ISBN: 978-1562477493

Split In Two: Keeping it Together When Your Parents Live Apart by Karen Buscemi (2009). Zest Books. ISBN: 978-0980073218

When Your Parents Split Up: How To Keep Yourself Together by Alys Swan-Jackson, Lynn Rosenfield, & Andy Cooke (1999). Sagebush Education Resources. ISBN: 978-0613823777

When Your Parents Divorce: A Handbook for Children Whose Parents Are Divorcing by Betty Clark (1998). Educational Media Corp. ISBN: 978-0932796899

Thank you for taking the time to read this book. I hope that you found it informative and helpful. If I or my office can be of help, please feel free to contact us at Israel Tel: (077) 200-8161 or U.S. Tel: (201) 696 – 3947. You can also schedule an appointment with us in one of our offices in Tel Aviv, Jerusalem, or Haifa.

Jay Hait, Adv.

www.IsraelDivorceLawyer.com

NOTES

NOTES

NOTES

Jay Hait, Adv.

<u>NOTES</u>

NOTES

NOTES

You can get an additional complimentary copy of this book!

If you found this book to be helpful and would like to share it with other people, I would be happy to provide you with an additional copy at no cost to you, anywhere in Israel. Just scan the QR code below or go to http://4ui.us/copies and fill in the order form and my office will send you the copy.

www.ingramcontent.com/pod-product-compliance
Lightning Source LLC
Chambersburg PA
CBHW021437170526
45164CB00001B/282